Tiffany, **Fresh Dew**

May God Bless
You, Grow you,
fulfill You
enormously,

Love

Elease

# Fresh Dew

Making Each Day Fresh for You

Elease Dobbs

Print information available on the last page.

Rev. date: 01/19/2016

# CONTENTS

# My journey

As a little girl I always love to read and write.
No matter what it was I would read it and take notes.
My favorite writer as a child was Judy Blume.
What an inspiration to know I could read something
cool, interesting and obtain knowledge
Hats off to you Judy!
Over my years I would just write and write never doing anything
with it, and then one day while praying, I asked God what's next.
God gave me direction "you have always had a gift of understanding
and writing, put it to use for others to enjoy and learn"
"Be truthful for their understanding and breakthrough"
Days later I gave birth to Fresh Dew.

# The Setup

Never realizing the setup of God, he blessed me with a manager
(Karen) that always critiqued my writing that she set me up with
a Mentor of which I give all kudos to for monitoring my writing
and helping me present it at all times with a spirit of Excellence.
Then he allowed me to meet and share my writing with so many
that encouraged me to continue to go forth with my writing.
It is an honor and a privilege to seek God and create writings
that will encourage, enlighten or inspire someone.

# Thanks to you

Thanks Hubby Leo for your patience when I would
stop doing everything immediately to write.
Thanks to all of my children for reading my pages daily.
Special thanks to my daughter Diamond for being my critic, you kept
me in order with your opinions and feedback concerning my writing.
Thank you Lady Kay for the confirmation of release and the many
tools, blessings, prayers and announcements you pushed my way.
Mom you gave me life, Dad (RIP) you always gave me
great things to read and your writing was so dynamic I
will one day release to the world in your honor. Grandma
(RIP) you said I was smart and brilliant and I could be
anything I wanted to be. I am walking in it now.

Madear aka (Mother) God gave me you even though
you did not birth me you molded me the way a
woman of God should be. I love you all.
Women of the Prayer Line thanks to you all for reading my Fresh
Dew daily I love you all for the love and encouragement.
Lastly, I give a special thanks to my Pastor Michael and Lady Eaddy
What would I do without you guys spiritual guidance. Pastor your
teachings, directness and anointing has surely applied nourishment
to my soul. Lady Eaddy you rock, I love you for being the example
of a mother, grandmother, woman of divine class. I will never
forget when you said to pray out loud so my children could see,
walk and talk like a lady. You sparked something inside me that
has allowed me to walk according to God. Thanks, I love you

Dear lord, never in a million years would I have
ever thought I would be doing this.
All I can say is thank you and continue to be
obedient to The Setup of my New Journey.
**Elease**

# Introducing Fresh Dew

Every morning when we wake up we should have a
Fresh Dew just like a fresh cup of hot coffee.
My goal with my Fresh Dew is to always keep
it fresh, inspiring and true for you.
I ask you to take this journey with me into something Fresh Daily.
I pray my books will relax, encourage, teach and
give you growth according to the God.
Ladies and Gents, I give you
**Fresh Dew**

# Gods Love

People in this world mostly likely will love based on how they receive
love, they go around picking and choosing who they will love,
This is the world's ways of loving, if you
love me I may love you back or
I don't know you so I can't love you

God loves regardless of who you are. There should be genuine
love flowing from one to another across the world. When
you have the love of God there are no stipulations,

many people believe they know what love is, but they don't.
If they have to pick and choose or
Wait on feelings they do not love with the
love of God, which is Agape love.

Everyone wants to be loved and most people want to love
others in return, but because of how they were raised
their perception of loving is based on feelings.

The time has come to change that, we all need to love
regardless and show genuine love daily because we have
the love of God who loves us no matter what.
We should be displaying the same across the universe.

If you do not love genuinely, it's time to research the word
of God and learn what love is. Do you want to know?

The Bible speaks many times about love, and what it is.
We need to grab our most important tool which is
the holy bible and search what is the true meaning
of love, so that we can walk in its daily,
Romans 8:37-39 says;
No, in all these things we are more than conquerors through him
who loved us. For I am sure that neither death nor life, nor angels
nor rulers, nor things present nor things to come, nor powers, nor
height nor depth, nor anything else in all creation, will be able
to separate us from the love of God in Christ Jesus our Lord.
Gods love teaches us to love regardless, the world
teaches us to love with exceptions.
Now whose way will you love?

Amen
Lady Elease

NOTES – WRITE DOWN YOUR THOUGHTS – DATE _____

_____

_____

_____

_____

_____

_____

_____

_____

## FIND A SCRIPTURE TO SPEAK TO YOUR THOUGHTS

_____

_____

_____

_____

_____

_____

_____

## WRITE A PRAYER

_____

_____

_____

_____

_____

_____

# Appeal to You

God is speaking to us people and the time
is NOW to adhere to his word.
Come out of your ways of the world and submit to him.
The battle is not ours.
So much is going on today, but if you bow
before him and stay there not wavering
You will be able to get through the tornados in life.
Hold on to Gods unchanging hands.
Young people this is so dearly on my heart
that this message is for you,
It is obvious the world's way does not work for you
Look around you, see the countless deaths daily.
I say seek him, and do it diligently
The time is now, call for peace in your life NOW!
Speak over your families and dwellings
The time is now to get in the Lords face,
Some of you may feel it is not cool,
No its not cool living according to the world
The word says;

**Romans 6:23 (KJV)**

**<sup>23</sup> For the wages of sin is death; but the gift of God
is eternal life through Jesus Christ our Lord.**

Stop and just think about what you have
gotten out of the ways of the world
Nothing!
We are losing our young children, women and men.
The attack is from Satan who you do not even know has setup camp

all around you to destroy devour and tear down.

I call forth order today in your life.

I ask you to stop right now whatever you are doing and repent

Accept God in your life; rekindle your relationship with him NOW.

Take back a hold of Jesus as your personal savior

believing he gave his life for all of us on that cross.

His dying was not in vain. I dare you in fact

I challenge you to stop right now and submit.

This is my appeal to you


Amen

Lady Elease

NOTES – WRITE DOWN YOUR THOUGHTS – DATE _____

_____

_____

_____

_____

_____

_____

_____

_____

FIND A SCRIPTURE TO SPEAK TO YOUR THOUGHTS

_____

_____

_____

_____

_____

_____

_____

WRITE A PRAYER

_____

_____

_____

_____

_____

_____

# Comfort in Scripture

Scriptures give us comfort and direction
So why do we go and tell someone of our situation
instead of reading the word of God?
Is it that we justify our situation by venting to people?
We need someone to talk to or
do we want a pity party?
What is our motive?
The best conversation we can have
is with God himself through prayer.
I am not saying some people don't have good direction.
However, our best results are from God.
Going to talk about our matters with others
does not give God the Glory, in fact
talking to others only delays our victory
Stop comforting yourselves in man
Give it to God
Start taking the initiative to speak your victory,
seal the deal
by reading and speaking the word
of God and then leave it in his hands.
No one can solve your matter but God
The word says;
Proverbs 3:5-6New International Version (NIV)
[5] Trust in the LORD with all your heart
and lean not on your own understanding;
[6] in all your ways submit to him,
and he will make your paths straight.
Remember there is comfort in scriptures not man
There is victory in God

Amen
Lady Elease

NOTES – WRITE DOWN YOUR THOUGHTS – DATE _____

_____

_____

_____

_____

_____

_____

_____

_____

FIND A SCRIPTURE TO SPEAK TO YOUR THOUGHTS

_____

_____

_____

_____

_____

_____

_____

WRITE A PRAYER

_____

_____

_____

_____

_____

_____

# Why is that?

Most people do not understand when you say
"I can't do anything until they hear from God"
you have to be obedient to God not man.
If you are obedient to God you will be obedient to everything else.
We must have the courage to take risk for God
Just like Esther did.
"If God is for us, who can be against us?" Romans 8:31b (NIV)
It is common sense to you to not rob a bank, because
you know you will go to jail *for* a long time
Which is a law of the world?
The bible tells us not to commit fornication or
adultery because it is a sin according to God.
Yet, I tend to think we would respect the law of
the world first before we would Gods.
Why is that?
Another example God will have you approach
someone for prayer or prophecy
and we back down because we do not know
them so we miss opportunity
in winning souls for God and getting him his GLORY.
Sometimes you will have to go against common sense,
against what others advise, even against what you
want to do in order to follow God's rules.
Often if we hear of someone talking about us
or possibly cheating with our mate,
without knowing them we will approach or
call to give them a piece of our mind.

Why is that?
Where is your obedience to the world or God?
Which can benefit you more?

Yes, God says to follow our laws on this earth, but he gets the Glory
In everything, not man.
You do not have to commit neither and God would get all the Glory
You have chosen to live right.
Stop taking risk on following the world's
way and disobeying God and his
Rules for us because we feel we can get away with them,
repent later then do it again.
Why is that?
Take the risk on being on obedient to God
and watch everything else fall in place

Amen
Lady Elease

NOTES – WRITE DOWN YOUR THOUGHTS – DATE _____

_____

_____

_____

_____

_____

_____

_____

_____

_____

FIND A SCRIPTURE TO SPEAK TO YOUR THOUGHTS

_____

_____

_____

_____

_____

_____

_____

WRITE A PRAYER

_____

_____

_____

_____

_____

_____

# Introduce or Re-Introduce

We have heard about or gotten to know
God at some point in our lives.
Do we really need him?
Is it a necessity to know him?
What if I use to know him but now I have gone astray from him?
What should I do?
These are the things that I have heard in my life from
others, in fact I have thought the same to myself.
There is one answer to all of the above and
that is to get to know God.
If you never have been on that one accord with him it is of
importance to introduce or re-introduce yourself to him.
Of course he already knows us all; however
he does not force himself on us.
If you want him then you must seek him for yourself.
It's a choice we make individually.
Just to pursue him better through prayer, read his Bible,
fellowship and learn with other Christians is all good.
However Jesus left us a message that said:
*"But your faith is not to rest in your effort, but
instead in God's ability to work in your life."*
*Jesus said it's like grapes on a vine. He is the main
vine and we are like the branches.*
*"Remain (or abide) in me and I will remain in you.
No branch can bear fruit by itself; it must remain in the vine.
Neither can you bear fruit unless you remain in me."[21]*

*"As the Father has loved me, so have I loved*
*you. Now remain in my love."*
If you do not know him, introduce yourself.
If you use to know him but haven't talked in a while re-introduce you
Time is of essence and he is waiting on YOU!


Amen
Lady Elease

NOTES – WRITE DOWN YOUR THOUGHTS – DATE _____

_____

_____

_____

_____

_____

_____

_____

_____

FIND A SCRIPTURE TO SPEAK TO YOUR THOUGHTS

_____

_____

_____

_____

_____

_____

_____

WRITE A PRAYER

_____

_____

_____

_____

_____

_____

# The true definition of a friend

You can search high and low for a friend once you
think you've found him or her, Boom!
Right in the face or straight to the back, to only
find out they were never your friend.

The question is how do you know when the friendship is true?

Should we receive new friendship?
If we have failed at many before?

Maybe we never had a friendship in the first place.
True friendship requires certain accountability factors.
Would a real friend tell your deepest secrets?
Shame you before others?
Never apologize when they've hurt your feelings?

Maybe that wasn't your friend
or perhaps you were the friend and that person wasn't.

How do you define true friendship?
According to God?

The bible says;
Hebrews 10:24-25 ESV

And let us consider how to stir up one another to love
and good works, not neglecting to meet together, as is
the habit of some, but encouraging one another, and
all the more as you see the day drawing near.


Real friends encourage one another and forgive one
another where there has been an offense.
Real friends acknowledge their wrong towards a friend


Are you a true friend?


If you are a friend or trying to be a friend remember
that friendship is genuine and from God.
Real friends fight for their friendship and they are genuine
from the heart always showing love and concern.
If you are a friend, have you been a friend to your friend?


As a friend you must


always want the best for your friend and this
would be the definition of a true friend.


Amen
Lady Elease

NOTES – WRITE DOWN YOUR THOUGHTS – DATE _____

_____

_____

_____

_____

_____

_____

_____

_____

FIND A SCRIPTURE TO SPEAK TO YOUR THOUGHTS

_____

_____

_____

_____

_____

_____

_____

WRITE A PRAYER

_____

_____

_____

_____

_____

_____

# elfie (what do you see?)

Take a good look at yourself
What does your portrait look like?
You are what you see
Every day is a selfie
Take a good look
When you speak
This represents your fear or confidence
when others hear or see you.
Your gestures and words
display loser or winner.
Who are you?
Winners embrace *opportunities*. Winners pursue *Miracles*.
Losers focus on their *problems*. Losers discuss their *obstacles*.
Losers focus on their *enemies' achievements*.
Losers adopt a *victim* mentality.
One choice is what you get.
Chose Winner or Loser.
Now look again in the mirror and tell me
Who do you see?
Are you a winner or loser?
Your selfie today is what you see in the mirror
***Philippians 1:6*** **Being confident of this
very thing, that he which has
begun a good work in you will perform
it until the day of Jesus Christ:**

God uses this Uncommon Dream to provide focus,
progression and enthusiasm.
Satan will develop a strategy to cloud this picture
and paralyze this Uncommon Dream.
You must recognize, so look in the mirror
See a strong woman or man of God
You are a winner!

AMEN
Lady Elease

NOTES – WRITE DOWN YOUR THOUGHTS – DATE _____

_____

_____

_____

_____

_____

_____

_____

_____

FIND A SCRIPTURE TO SPEAK TO YOUR THOUGHTS

_____

_____

_____

_____

_____

_____

_____

WRITE A PRAYER

_____

_____

_____

_____

_____

_____

# It is time

Hold your head up
Walk forward knowing you are who God created.
You're bold, unique, creative, and special and most of all favored.
Because you have the confidence in knowing
God will do just what his word says.
So many of us are afraid to say who we are and what we want in this
lifetime. Why are you shameful to mention to others the impossible?
Who cares if they laugh or talk about you?
You serve the great King of All.
He has spread out before you
his will for your life, don't allow others lack of belief discourage you.
Didn't he say you could have the desires of your heart?
The word says in;
Hebrews 10:35-36
therefore do not throw away your confidence, which has a great
reward. For you have need of endurance, so that when you have
done the will of God you may receive what is promised.
Attention over here, it is time to realize who you are
and who you have you have backing you up.
Stop shying away from your goals and dreams, go get
them with all the confidence that you can dig up.
It's time!

Amen
Lady Elease

NOTES – WRITE DOWN YOUR THOUGHTS – DATE _____

_____

_____

_____

_____

_____

_____

_____

FIND A SCRIPTURE TO SPEAK TO YOUR THOUGHTS

_____

_____

_____

_____

_____

_____

WRITE A PRAYER

_____

_____

_____

_____

_____

# To War Is To Have Faith

To war is to have faith.
No matter what happens you still have faith in God

It appears, it looks
But your faith still lies deep.
So much belief
you can see the victory ahead.

To war is to have faith
You continuously trust and believe
You call on God to show you the way
Never pausing, never doubting

You have all the ammunition you need,
Prayer is the key;

Hear my prayer, O Lord; listen to my cry for mercy. In the day of my
trouble I will call to you, for you will answer me' (Psalm 86:6-7).

The word assures you
Restores your confidence
Guides and soothes you

Don't lose your faith
Without faith your war is loss
God is with you at all times
To war is to have faith
To win the war is to trust that God is with you at all times.

Amen
Lady Elease

NOTES – WRITE DOWN YOUR THOUGHTS – DATE _____

_____

_____

_____

_____

_____

_____

_____

_____

FIND A SCRIPTURE TO SPEAK TO YOUR THOUGHTS

_____

_____

_____

_____

_____

_____

_____

WRITE A PRAYER

_____

_____

_____

_____

_____

_____

# A Rush in a Hurry

Your moving so fast
cannot be late;
everything is hurry-hurry-hurry.
There's never enough time,
you're always running late.
Behind schedule, caught by the tardy bell is truly a factor in your life.
There is never an on time moment,
Never a time you're not in a hurry.
Never a time you're not rushing,
always Late-late-late!
The story of your life is never having enough time in your day.
Everything has become a schedule;
our work, family time, social life and chores are time set.
If the time rolls past, we just missed that too.
Having more time is something we all want,
but even with 24 hours a day we're
still A Rush in A Hurry
Exodus 5:13
and the taskmasters forced them to hurry, saying, and "Fulfill
your work, your daily quota, as when there was straw.
Remember to be anxious for nothing thus saith the Lord.
Let's pump our brakes and slow down, stop rushing
and don't be in a hurry. All you can't accomplish today
there's always tomorrow if the Lord willing.

Amen
Lady Elease

NOTES – WRITE DOWN YOUR THOUGHTS – DATE _____

_____

_____

_____

_____

_____

_____

_____

_____

FIND A SCRIPTURE TO SPEAK TO YOUR THOUGHTS

_____

_____

_____

_____

_____

_____

_____

WRITE A PRAYER

_____

_____

_____

_____

_____

_____

# Evaluate your Display

Who do they see when they see you?

Many times we do not have a clear visual of
which people see when we enter a room,

What about when you speak.
Do we run off at the mouth not guarding our words?

A lot of people do not know what onlookers
see when they come on display.

As a woman or man of God we are on display
the minute we claim being saved.
"People are paying attention"

You can go all week and very few will approach
you concerning the display they see.
Philippians 2:14-15
Do all things without grumbling or questioning, that you
may be blameless and innocent, children of God without
blemish in the midst of a crooked and twisted generation,
among whom you shine as lights in the world,

Remember once you step out of your door you are on display.
Your character is being examined.

You now know that the most important aspect
of your character is being on display.
Everyone that see and hear you from this
point on will watch and judge you.
Always make sure you evaluate self before your display tumbles down.

Amen

Lady Elease

NOTES – WRITE DOWN YOUR THOUGHTS – DATE _____

_____

_____

_____

_____

_____

_____

_____

_____

FIND A SCRIPTURE TO SPEAK TO YOUR THOUGHTS

_____

_____

_____

_____

_____

_____

_____

WRITE A PRAYER

_____

_____

_____

_____

_____

_____

# Let there be peace

Romans 14:19
Let us therefore make every effort to do what
leads to peace and to mutual edification.

Let there be peace in all you do according to God.
You are the holder of your peace, never allows
anyone to take this from you.

Every day, you must hold your peace close to your
heart. At any moment peace can be stolen.
Be cautious, be alert at all times

Peace can be taken by anyone, your spouse,
workplace, children, friends or random people.

The further your peace gets from you the more you
lose control, the quicker you will explode.
Boom off it goes!

But before this happens, breathe,
Grad a hold of your peace and never let it go in any situation.

There will be many times you will have to breathe and shut up, it
can become a struggle, just hold your peace tight and never let it go.

Make every effort to keep your peace, its well
worth it don't let anyone steal your peace.

Chaos swirls around in every which way. Peace, stillness, infinite
self lives within you, especially in times that seem so hard.

You can make it, so stand up and
stretch your arms forward, pull back
embracing yourself tight, now breathe.
Kneel down, fold your hands and bow your head.
Pray and get up.

Now you still have your peace because all your
concerns are placed in the master's hand.
Even in those moments where peace seems impossible.
Remember Jesus said "peace I leave you"
Therefore you have peace in everything.

Amen
Lady Elease

NOTES – WRITE DOWN YOUR THOUGHTS – DATE _____

FIND A SCRIPTURE TO SPEAK TO YOUR THOUGHTS

WRITE A PRAYER

# I'm smiling

I'm smiling because my smiles tells me there is a brighter day coming

Things may look sour right now,
I smile about it anyway
I had a bad day,
yet I still smiled.

Things didn't go through for me the way I
planned and I didn't stop smiling,

As we live this life there will a many times it doesn't work in our favor.

What do we do whine and cry about it?
No, you smile about it anyway.
A smile goes a long way and it tells Satan face on
"I'm not giving up, there will be better days"

Ephesians 1:18-20 "I pray also that the eyes of your heart may
be enlightened in order that you may know the hope to which
he has called you, the riches of his glorious inheritance in the
saints and his incomparably great power for us who believe.
That power is like the working of his mighty strength which
he exerted in Christ when he raised him from the dead."

I'm smiling anyway to always be prepared for whatever life
brings me. A smile is strength, energy to carry on.

Just like the song says;
"Great is Thy faithfulness" which speaks of "Strength
for today and bright hope for tomorrow."

Tomorrow will be a better day so Smile

Amen,
Lady Elease

NOTES – WRITE DOWN YOUR THOUGHTS – DATE _____

_____

_____

_____

_____

_____

_____

_____

_____

_____

FIND A SCRIPTURE TO SPEAK TO YOUR THOUGHTS

_____

_____

_____

_____

_____

_____

_____

WRITE A PRAYER

_____

_____

_____

_____

_____

_____

# Pretender

Who are we?
Inside and out is what should match.
Are you one way on the inside?
Another on outside
Do you have to out on to fit in?
Who are you?
Matthew 15:7 NIV
You hypocrites! Isaiah was right when he prophesied about you:
"'These people honor me with their lips,
but their hearts are far from me.
Is this what you have God say to you on judgment day?
Do you not care that you falsely represent his kingdom?
Daily people go about their own lives
Living their own ways
Once assemble they become someone new.
Why not be who you really are.
God knows us all so no need to pretend.
We are either gone live according to this world or according to God.
I now ask "who are you"
We seem to think we have mastered how to fool man
Because they are not with us 24/7 we do as we please
Going about living like a heathen.
Once assemble with the people of God we
are now holier than though.
Our insides love everything concerning God
But because we allow flesh to rule our outside is
taking your inside straight to HELL.

Time to stop pretending,
Make the change,
Get the inside to control the outside so that
they match accordingly to God
Let your words on the outside match your
thoughts and heart on the inside
*And I will give you a new heart, and a new spirit I will put within you.*
*And I will remove the heart of stone from your*
*flesh and give you a heart of flesh.*
*And I will put my Spirit within you, and cause you to walk in my statutes*
*and be careful to obey my rules.* Ezekiel 36:26-27

Amen,
Lady Elease

NOTES — WRITE DOWN YOUR THOUGHTS — DATE _____

_____

_____

_____

_____

_____

_____

_____

_____

FIND A SCRIPTURE TO SPEAK TO YOUR THOUGHTS

_____

_____

_____

_____

_____

_____

_____

WRITE A PRAYER

_____

_____

_____

_____

_____

_____

# Your Vision is waiting

You have to say it,

then you have to mean it.

You have to want it,

then you must make plans to go get it.

Stop just talking,

talk is cheap.

Action speaks louder than words.

Are you still sitting there?

Get up go plant your seeds.

Oh yeah, they will not grow if you do not water them.

Here is the recipe to growing your HARVEST.

Your source

Your faith

Your trust

Your foundation

Your vision

Your goal

Your plan

Your prayer life

Your meditation on the word

Your action

All you need is these few ingredients and before you know it
your vision will have manifested right before your eyes.

James 2:14,26 (NKJV)

[14] What *does it* profit, my brethren, if someone says he has
faith but does not have works? Can faith save him?

[26] For as the body without the spirit is dead,
so faith without works is dead also.
Now get up and get to work,
Your vision is waiting.

Amen

Lady Elease

NOTES – WRITE DOWN YOUR THOUGHTS – DATE _____

_____

_____

_____

_____

_____

_____

_____

_____

_____

FIND A SCRIPTURE TO SPEAK TO YOUR THOUGHTS

_____

_____

_____

_____

_____

_____

_____

WRITE A PRAYER

_____

_____

_____

_____

_____

_____

# What is the purpose to be Envious?

Have you ever experienced this, you being
envious or others being envious of you?

Either way being envious is tiresome, a WASTE
of time and nothing but jealousy.

In this world there will always be people who are better off
or doing less than you in at least one area. They will always
feel envious of you as well as you being envious of them.

Being envious is time consuming; allowing it to get in your
head will make you spend lots of time feeling angry and bitter
towards others because they have something you don't.

Not a good way to live your life, in fact very miserable.

I ask you today, what is the purpose of being envious of someone?

Time to stop being envious, it is nothing but jealousy,
another way for Satan to control your emotions.

James 3:16 says, for where jealousy and selfish ambition
exist, there will be disorder and every vile practice.

The key to being happy in your season of life is to be
happy for others, stay less informed, build stronger
relationships that you as well as others can be true towards
one another and most of all learn to love/like yourself.

With these keys applied to your life No longer
will you worry about the next person?
Remember there is no good outcome in being envious
so again, what is the purpose of being envious?

If you are envious seek God.
Because of his faithfulness he will find a way
for you to escape your emotions.

Amen
Lady Elease

NOTES – WRITE DOWN YOUR THOUGHTS – DATE _____

_____

_____

_____

_____

_____

_____

_____

_____

FIND A SCRIPTURE TO SPEAK TO YOUR THOUGHTS

_____

_____

_____

_____

_____

_____

_____

WRITE A PRAYER

_____

_____

_____

_____

_____

_____

# A love like mines

We all want to be loved, but do we know what love is?
We turn love on and off like water.

Just pause for a moment and think about what love really is to you.

In this life there are two types of love.
The first one is; "agape." This love is represented by God's
love for us. It is a non-partial, sacrificial love probably best
exemplified by God's provision for our rebellion:
The second one is love according to this world which
is emotional feeling, compassion and conditional. This
type of love is short lived and mostly temporary.

The Bible shares that love is from God. In fact, the Bible says
"God is love." Love is one of the primary characteristics of
God. Likewise, God has endowed us with the capacity for love,
since we are created in His image. This capacity for love is one
of the ways in which we are "created in the image of God.

To have a love like mines is to have an unchanging love, sacrifice
love, no matter what you do love. This is the love I have from
God and this is the love I strive daily to give to everyone.

How many of us can say we give this?
Let's love according to God and pour that true love onto others daily

Remembering the greatest love of from the scripture John 3:16; "For God so loved the world, that He gave His only begotten Son, that whoever believes in Him should not perish, but has eternal life."

If you want to spread your love and receive this
love then you need a love like mines.
Love the way God loves you and that is agape love.

Amen
Lady Elease

NOTES – WRITE DOWN YOUR THOUGHTS – DATE _____

_____
_____
_____
_____
_____
_____
_____
_____
_____

FIND A SCRIPTURE TO SPEAK TO YOUR THOUGHTS

_____
_____
_____
_____
_____
_____
_____

WRITE A PRAYER

_____
_____
_____
_____
_____
_____

# Stamp Your Mark

You are here for purpose
Do not live in vain
Everyone has a reason for being on this earth.
Time to Stamp Your Mark!

The reason for our life here on this earth is to learn
about self which is our purpose according to God.
Do you know yourself? If not the time has come to discover YOU.

Who is this person, that person are you. Self is that very real
part of you that wants to bring forth their purpose. Your self is
the one who should Stamp a Mark before leaving this earth.

However, it is only when you become aware of whom
you are, that you can go on and stamp your mark.

Have you started stamping your mark?
If you left today will people benefit from your life?

Time to start stamping just like Jesus, Moses and
Abraham; they all left a Mark on this earth for us all.
Do not allow your living to be in vain.

The word says, Matthew 5:13-16 ESV

"You are the salt of the earth, but if salt has lost its taste, how shall its saltiness be restored? It is no longer good for anything except to be thrown out and trampled under people's feet. "You are the light of the world. A city set on a hill cannot be hidden. Nor do people light a lamp and put it under a basket, but on a stand, and it gives light to all in the house. In the same way, let your light shine before others, so that they may see your good works and give glory to your Father who is in heaven.

Time to Stamp Your Mark!

Amen,
Lady Elease

NOTES – WRITE DOWN YOUR THOUGHTS – DATE _____

_____

_____

_____

_____

_____

_____

_____

_____

FIND A SCRIPTURE TO SPEAK TO YOUR THOUGHTS

_____

_____

_____

_____

_____

_____

_____

WRITE A PRAYER

_____

_____

_____

_____

_____

_____

# Everything is to be celebrated

Never take life for granted. From good too bad you should celebrate.

From the small things to the great big things, let's celebrate!

Have you ever started late for an appointment and God still
blessed you to arrive on time by giving you all the green
lights, a minimum of stop signs and pedestrians?
What about favor to arrive before everyone else and to think
you were the running late. This deserves a celebration.

Some more things to celebrate that people may look at as bad; you
lost your job but the company gave you a severance package, car
accident that totaled your car and you walked away without a scratch.
Lastly, you never had love by your immediate family; you
met a friend whose family loves you like their own.
These are celebrations.

To celebrate is the simple act of being thankful,
appreciative or feeling blessed.

1 Corinthians 10:31 (KJV)
Whether therefore ye eat, or drink, or whatsoever
ye do, do all to the glory of God.

Let's remember to celebrate daily, because every day is a celebration.

Amen
Lady Elease

NOTES – WRITE DOWN YOUR THOUGHTS – DATE _____

_____

_____

_____

_____

_____

_____

_____

_____

_____

FIND A SCRIPTURE TO SPEAK TO YOUR THOUGHTS

_____

_____

_____

_____

_____

_____

_____

WRITE A PRAYER

_____

_____

_____

_____

_____

_____

# Moving at a steady pace

Stop!

Why are you dragging alone, nothing will ever
get done with you moving like a turtle.

Pick up your speed; add some pep to your step. The quicker
you move the sooner you can get done and move to the next.

You are not on your time it is the Lord's time.
Being slow is not a part of the kingdom.

Come on get it done, think of the word of
God to move at a steady pace.

Ephesians 5:15-17 ESV
Look carefully then how you walk, not as unwise but as wise,
making the best use of the time, because the days are evil. Therefore
do not be foolish, but understand what the will of the Lord is.

The word of God gives you life and strength.
No time for playing around for no one knows
when their clock will run out.

I tell you today if you have tasks, visions or assignments to get
done according to God move at a steady pace to get it done.

If you have goals and dreams to accomplish that you have talked out with God and he said it's his will for your life, you should be moving at a steady pace to get them done.

Can you imagine how quickly things would start to happen if you got up and took care of your business today?

Remember each day is an accomplishment if you move at a steady pace by doing things daily towards your assignments from God or your personal goals.

Come on let's move at a steady pace, the next task or dream awaits you.

Amen
Lady Elease

NOTES – WRITE DOWN YOUR THOUGHTS – DATE _____

_____
_____
_____
_____
_____
_____
_____
_____
_____

FIND A SCRIPTURE TO SPEAK TO YOUR THOUGHTS

_____
_____
_____
_____
_____
_____
_____

WRITE A PRAYER

_____
_____
_____
_____
_____
_____

# Break Yourself

1 Corinthians 10:13
No temptation has seized you except what is common to man.
And God is faithful; he will not let you be tempted beyond
what you can bear. But when you are tempted, he will also
provide a way out so that you can stand up under it.

A lot of times we as people stay in an addictive relationship
because the person fulfills us in some kind of exciting way, either
emotionally or sexually, and we become blind of true facts.

We either can't imagine our lives without the person or
we are afraid we will never find someone else to make
us feel the way they did emotional or physical.

Not only can we become addictive to a person we
also can be addictive to things and places which
can hinder us from going forward in life.

It takes awhile for us to finally realize that we have an addiction.
Sometimes it gets so bad we don't even
realize that something is wrong.
Until that one day we realize it's time to break
ourselves because we are addicted!

Addictions are things which are inherently
dangerous for us, a habit we cannot break.
Instead of bringing us happiness, it causes us much dismay and hurt.

People who are addicted can be mentally or physically
damaged internal and external. If you know you or someone
else is acting this way then it is time to break yourself!

The only solution to have a complete deliverance to an
addiction is to seek the Lord by Prayer and his words.
Yes, they have Doctor and counselors but
the true healing is from God.

Break yourself!

Amen
Lady Elease

NOTES – WRITE DOWN YOUR THOUGHTS – DATE _____

_____
_____
_____
_____
_____
_____
_____
_____

FIND A SCRIPTURE TO SPEAK TO YOUR THOUGHTS

_____
_____
_____
_____
_____
_____
_____

WRITE A PRAYER

_____
_____
_____
_____
_____
_____

# Yesterday is Gone, Today is a New Day, Fight!

When you talk of things of the past, do they
still sadden you or make you cry?
If so you are still playing victim to the past of your life.
The time has come for you to FIGHT!

If you are here to tell the story, then it should
no longer have an effect on you.
Your past journeys in life are meant to deliver and heal someone.
It is our duty to give GLORY and honor to the Almighty God.

Why do you sit and dwell on the past? Pity parties are for the birds.
You should be telling someone your story to give them a
short-cut to overcoming the same or similar situation.
Before you tell your story again go and get delivered, get
healed so that you can help someone get the victory.

Isaiah 43:18-19
"Forget the former things;
do not dwell on the past.
See, I am doing a new thing!
Now it springs up; do you not perceive it?
I am making a way in the desert
and streams in the wasteland." (NIV)

Stop letting your past continue to hold you bound.
Take the key back from the strong hold and unlock yourself.
It is time to Fight and Win starting today.

Yesterday is Gone, Today is a New Day.

Fight!

Amen
Lady Elease

NOTES – WRITE DOWN YOUR THOUGHTS – DATE _____

_____
_____
_____
_____
_____
_____
_____
_____
_____

FIND A SCRIPTURE TO SPEAK TO YOUR THOUGHTS

_____
_____
_____
_____
_____
_____
_____

WRITE A PRAYER

_____
_____
_____
_____
_____
_____

# Feels like your losing

Have you ever been moving right along with your
hopes, dreams or goals then all of a sudden just
like a tire losing air your journey goes flat.

It's like everything seems to be going downhill, your only
blame is the devil, he has to be the one behind this.

Every time you get close to your dream or goal, out of nowhere,
BAM Something gets in your way, and the pause button is pushed.

Why Lord, why?
What did I do to deserve this?
I live, forgive, pray and tithe.
What is going on, why do I feel like I'm losing?

The word says "Be strong and courageous. Do not fear or be
in dread of them, for it is the LORD your God who goes with
you. He will not leave you or forsake you." Deuteronomy 3:16

Just because all seems loss does not mean you are losing.
In fact it means you are gaining. So many things try to
interrupt or detour you from pressing forward.

Here's a small pointer;
never give up on your hopes, dreams or goals. The interruptions
in life are to make sure you are leaning on the total help of the
Lord; it is also that extra push you need to say it was all worth it!

Remember to always keep pressing, keep moving, you're not losing.

Amen
Lady Elease

NOTES – WRITE DOWN YOUR THOUGHTS – DATE _____

_____

_____

_____

_____

_____

_____

_____

_____

_____

FIND A SCRIPTURE TO SPEAK TO YOUR THOUGHTS

_____

_____

_____

_____

_____

_____

_____

WRITE A PRAYER

_____

_____

_____

_____

_____

_____

# Life

Psalm 138:3
"In the day when I cried out, you answered me, and
made me bold with strength in my soul."

Life is a precious, valuable source that we all get. Each life
has a time and date stamped for arrival and departure.

There are ups and downs, turnarounds and splits. When
it comes to life you never know how you will land.

The safest landing in life is to have God present. When
facing life challenges you cannot do it alone. Do not think
you can go around single handedly and live your life.

You and I both need God in any situation
for the many challenges to come.
The one help we need will always be there for us, so remember
to always turn to the all-powerful Creator God.
His strength and renewal can help us face our many
fears and the impossible life challenges.

God's awe-inspiring creation is far more worthy and compelling.
This creation is called life there is no outlet to step over
God's will for your life to enjoy, reap, sow and overcome.

Remember these things I say to you before
you make a wrong move on life.
Matthew 6:33 tells us to "Seek first His kingdom and His
righteousness"; you want to know how of course?

Well, first we get somewhere daily calling on Jesus to come into our
lives; from then on we have daily conversation through Jesus to God.

From that day forward, never make a move without
consulting God, Your life depends on it!

Amen,
Lady Elease

NOTES – WRITE DOWN YOUR THOUGHTS – DATE _____

_____

_____

_____

_____

_____

_____

_____

_____

FIND A SCRIPTURE TO SPEAK TO YOUR THOUGHTS

_____

_____

_____

_____

_____

_____

_____

WRITE A PRAYER

_____

_____

_____

_____

_____

_____

# Get a hold of yourself.

Life is about peace and comfort the word told us when Jesus said; he had to go for now but he would leave us with peace and comfort.

John 14:27
Peace I leave with you; my peace I give you. I do not give to you as the world gives. Do not let your hearts be troubled and do not be afraid.

So many of us run with our heads cut off by too much multitasking, extracurricular, cluttered living and always moving at a fast pace. Is this healthy is this all worth it? I don't think so.

We must be about our business. However, there is order, peace and comfort that come with that. Slow down a moment and take a breather. Moving, rushing and always in a hurry deteriorates our external and internal being.

Moving too fast can take a toll on our life. Hurrying daily has an effect on us mentally and physically... Once again slow down, and remember Rome wasn't built in a day.

Time to get a hold of yourself before life passes you by.

Amen,
Lady Elease

NOTES – WRITE DOWN YOUR THOUGHTS – DATE _____

_____

_____

_____

_____

_____

_____

_____

_____

FIND A SCRIPTURE TO SPEAK TO YOUR THOUGHTS

_____

_____

_____

_____

_____

_____

_____

WRITE A PRAYER

_____

_____

_____

_____

_____

_____

# Your Support System

We are each other's support system,
No one can do it by themselves.
It may look this way, but you are not alone.
We depend on each other being loyal to Gods kingdom.
"Two are better than one...For if they fall, the one
will lift up his fellow: but woe to him
that is alone when he falleth; for he hath not another
to help him up," (Ecclesiastes 4:9-10).
When someone is genuine, honest and loyal to
your journey, this is your support system
Do not take it person this is your support
system when someone gives you
feedback and rocks with you in good or bad times.
When you are being corrected, directed, protected by
someone this is a sign of you not being alone.
Walking alone, doing it all by yourself and shutting
people out really leads you nowhere.
Yes, you can rise to the top by yourself,
but what good is it to be alone?
A good support system that seeks God and is truly loyal
to him first will support you truly from their heart.
Although, they are hard to find like a diamond
in a hay stack they are out there.
To link with a good support system seeks God
diligently to show you who is real.
Make sure you understand and have the wisdom
until God builds your support system

by watching and praying.

In order words two eyes of God are better than one.

No matter what know that everyone needs someone,

there is no such thing as "I can do it all by myself".

If you are the one who wants to travel uphill

alone, it is a tough and lonely road.

Get your support system in place and never leave home without it!

Amen

Lady Elease

NOTES – WRITE DOWN YOUR THOUGHTS – DATE _____

_____

_____

_____

_____

_____

_____

_____

_____

_____

FIND A SCRIPTURE TO SPEAK TO YOUR THOUGHTS

_____

_____

_____

_____

_____

_____

_____

WRITE A PRAYER

_____

_____

_____

_____

_____

_____

# APart, Not APart

You may have come into this world with a lot of baggage based on your race, color, environment, parents and ancestors this only means you are APart, but Not APart.

Just because the situation looks bad doesn't
mean it has to stay that way.
Jesus died for that reason alone.
You now have choices, if you were born poor you can be rich, if you were never shown love it's out there waiting for you. If family members all die from diseases you can be disease free and if generational curses have traveled in your family for decades they can now be broken.

Jeremiah 29:11 ESV
For I know the plans I have for you, declares the Lord, plans for welfare and not for evil, to give you a future and a hope.

The word of God assures us that just because we were born into something it is not a foundation permanently for us.

Stop holding self back because of what has
happened in the past to your family.
Aim high and don't look back.
So what if everyone in your life has been a failure you can be a success if you put your trust in the hands of the Lord.

Remember you must believe and have faith in Jesus
who died for you to now have choices.

Don't listen when they say such and such had the
same dreams and ended up nowhere.
Let them know the difference is you trust God for your life
and his word says you can have the desires of your heart.

Yes you are APart, but you do not have to be
APart of the mishaps in your generation.

Stop comparing yourself to things that mean
nothing to your journey ahead.

Know that you are APart of an awesome God who has given his only
begotten son to sacrifice for you so that you would have choices.

Amen
Lady Elease

NOTES – WRITE DOWN YOUR THOUGHTS – DATE _____

_____

_____

_____

_____

_____

_____

_____

_____

FIND A SCRIPTURE TO SPEAK TO YOUR THOUGHTS

_____

_____

_____

_____

_____

_____

_____

WRITE A PRAYER

_____

_____

_____

_____

_____

_____

# A little more EXTRA!

Do more than what is really expected of you.

Does not the potter have the right to make out of the
same lump of clay some pottery for noble purposes
and some for common use? (Romans 9:21)

We are all unique, as God went a little more extra each
day he added to his 6 day completion of the world.

We must follow him as an example to get things done.

Go a little extra today to get it finished.

You want a business, to write a book, build a house or
create a design you must do something extra.

A lot of time our effort is in the wrong place. Focus on the
importance that will please God and get you closer to the finish line.

Remember each time you complete something
your closer than you were yesterday.

Philippians 4:13 - I can do all things through
Christ which strengthened me.

Sometimes you have to go the extra mile
(or at least finish the first mile)

In all you do,
do a little EXTRA.

Amen,
Lady Elease

NOTES – WRITE DOWN YOUR THOUGHTS – DATE _____

_____

_____

_____

_____

_____

_____

_____

FIND A SCRIPTURE TO SPEAK TO YOUR THOUGHTS

_____

_____

_____

_____

_____

_____

_____

WRITE A PRAYER

_____

_____

_____

_____

_____

# I could only imagine

Many say they control their own life, they are fortunate
because of them. Some even feel they can make it without him,
that it's not important to have a relationship with him.

Philippians 3:8 says;
Yes everything else is worthless when compared with the infinite
value of knowing Christ Jesus my Lord. For his sake I have discarded
everything else, counting it all as garbage, so that I could gain Christ

This is so true to me because I would rather have Jesus than to
have the things of the world, than to be friends or in company
with the people of the world who do not accept him or do
not acknowledge him, most of all do not praise Him.

I could only imagine the life that I would live
without having Jesus in my life.

Imagine not being able to call upon God
and talk to him in the wee hours.
What would you do, would you rather have the world,
would you rather have man to talk to you?

This is a very important question that's why I'm asking
you. I can only imagine my life without Jesus, to be
a terrible, loss, empty and destined for hell.

I am concerned about your life so I'm asking you
could you imagine your life without Jesus.

We learn from an early age to be self-sufficient and allow this
thinking to carry over in all walks of our lives. And because we
are a nation of "fix it yourselfers", many of us feel we can handle
life issues under our own steam and power without spiritual
help. With this thinking we are isolated, self-dependent and
our sins will continue to multiply and become impossible to
repair by ourselves. This mentality separates us from God.

Without Jesus we cannot get to God.
The word tells us this is the only way.
I could only imagine never getting to know God because
I never got to know Jesus, What about you?

I could only imagine we learn from an early age to be self-sufficient
and allow this thinking to carry over in all walks of our lives. And
because we are a nation of "fix it yourselfers", many of us feel we
can handle life issues under our own steam and power without
spiritual help. With this thinking we are isolated, self-dependent
and our sins will continue to multiply and become impossible
to repair by ourselves. This mentality separates us from God.

Amen
Lady Elease

NOTES – WRITE DOWN YOUR THOUGHTS – DATE _____

_____
_____
_____
_____
_____
_____
_____
_____
_____

FIND A SCRIPTURE TO SPEAK TO YOUR THOUGHTS

_____
_____
_____
_____
_____
_____
_____

WRITE A PRAYER

_____
_____
_____
_____
_____
_____

# Gods Groups

Groups are put together for networking
There are worldly groups
There are Godly groups.

To God be the glory for his groups that
are ordered and specially designed by him himself

When chosen for Gods specialties
We must come hungry, bold and ready

Settling for less,
Putting forth little effort
is not an option.

Remember the Glory is for God
So give it your best!

One cannot build and finish by themselves, it takes two
or more always, Lets take our places and go for it!

Whatever task we have been assigned
stay together and help one another,
as the word says "two are better than one"

"Two are better than one; because they have
a good reward for their labour.
For if they fall, the one will lift up his fellow:
but woe to him that is alone when he falleth; for he hath
not another to help him up," (Ecclesiastes 4:9-10).

Everyone comes with a special gift, skill and knowledge.
Listening, learning and understanding one another are a true
fact of a great outcome, which is the Glory to our King.

Press forward to network for God
You are a part of Gods Group.

Amen
Lady Elease

NOTES – WRITE DOWN YOUR THOUGHTS – DATE _____

_____

_____

_____

_____

_____

_____

_____

_____

FIND A SCRIPTURE TO SPEAK TO YOUR THOUGHTS

_____

_____

_____

_____

_____

_____

_____

WRITE A PRAYER

_____

_____

_____

_____

_____

_____

# Be thankful

Giving thanks is pleasing to God
It's the small things that count.
Show God the thankfulness for the little,
things, lack of and being without.

These gestures bring bigger and better according to God there is no
set amount of time, just be thankful just like Daniel in the bible.

Daniel 6:10 - "Now when Daniel knew that the writing was signed,
he went into his house; and his windows being open in his chamber
toward Jerusalem, he kneeled upon his knees three times a day,
and prayed, and gave thanks before his God, as he did aforetime.

No matter what, be consistent
Praise him anyhow,
Regardless of the outcome,
Keep smiling
Praise him anyhow.
Joy comes in the morning

We need to be thankful
for the job, not mad for the pay.
Be appreciative we have a house
and not upset where it's located

Enter into his gates with thanksgiving,
and into his courts with praise:
be thankful unto him, and bless his name. Psalm 100:4 (KJV)


Every morning you rise,
Every night before you sleep
Be thankful


Be thankful you have two good legs to walk money for public
transportation and stop complaining you do not have a car.


So many of us spend more time complaining, and
then thanking God for what we currently have.


We are never satisfied if things are not going our way.


Reality check things could be a lot worse, be thankful.


Amen
Lady Elease

NOTES – WRITE DOWN YOUR THOUGHTS – DATE _____

_____

_____

_____

_____

_____

_____

_____

_____

FIND A SCRIPTURE TO SPEAK TO YOUR THOUGHTS

_____

_____

_____

_____

_____

_____

_____

WRITE A PRAYER

_____

_____

_____

_____

_____

_____

# The true definition of a friend

You can search high and low for a friend once you
think you've found him or her, Boom!
Right in the face or straight to the back, to only
find out they were never your friend.

The question is how do you know when the friendship is true?

Should we receive new friendship?
if we have failed at many before?

Maybe we never had a friendship in the first place.
True friendship requires certain accountability factors.
Would a real friend tell your deepest secrets?
Shame you before others?
Never apologize when they've hurt your feelings?

Maybe that wasn't your friend
or perhaps you were the friend and that person wasn't.

How do you define true friendship?
According to God?

The bible says;
Hebrews 10:24-25 ESV

And let us consider how to stir up one another to love
and good works, not neglecting to meet together, as is
the habit of some, but encouraging one another, and
all the more as you see the day drawing near.

Real friends encourage one another and forgive one
another where there has been an offense.
Real friends acknowledge their wrong towards a friend

Are you a true friend?

If you are a friend or trying to be a friend remember
that friendship is genuine and from God.

Real friends fight for their friendship and they are genuine
from the heart always showing love and concern.

If you are a friend, have you been a friend to your friend?

As a friend you must
always want the best for your friend and this
would be the definition of a true friend.

Amen
Lady Elease

NOTES – WRITE DOWN YOUR THOUGHTS – DATE _____

_____

_____

_____

_____

_____

_____

_____

_____

FIND A SCRIPTURE TO SPEAK TO YOUR THOUGHTS

_____

_____

_____

_____

_____

_____

_____

WRITE A PRAYER

_____

_____

_____

_____

_____

_____

# Time to find out who you really are.

Who are you?
Fiction or Non-Fiction.
The truth or a lie.

There is a saying "it takes courage to find out who you really are"
Are you brave enough?

Do you really want to find out?

You must press daily to be who God has designed you to
be. Yes it's your choice, but being who God has chosen
is approved and all you have to do is live by it.
When you find out who you are according to
God, walking in confidence daily, you need not
to be a shame. You are stamped approved.

The word says;
2 Timothy 2:15 ESV
Do your best to present yourself to God as one approved, a worker
who has no need to be ashamed, rightly handling the word.

When you can walk with confidence and rep the
Word of God then you know who you are.

If you are going about your life doing what you want to do, not caring who sees you, then you do not know who you are and the time has come for you to find out!

Are you ready?

Amen

Lady Elease

NOTES – WRITE DOWN YOUR THOUGHTS – DATE _____

_____

_____

_____

_____

_____

_____

_____

_____

FIND A SCRIPTURE TO SPEAK TO YOUR THOUGHTS

_____

_____

_____

_____

_____

_____

_____

WRITE A PRAYER

_____

_____

_____

_____

_____

_____

# Your Support System

We are each other's support system,
No one can do it by themselves.
It may look this way, but you are not alone.
We depend on each other being loyal to Gods kingdom.

"Two are better than one...For if they fall, the one will lift up
his fellow: but woe to him that is alone when he falleth; for
he hath not another to help him up," (Ecclesiastes 4:9-10).

When someone is genuine, honest and loyal to
your journey, this is your support system

Do not take it personal when someone gives you
corrections or opinions, receive their feedback.
Know that this person will rock with you in good or bad times.

When you are being corrected, directed, protected by
someone this is a sign of you not being alone.
Walking alone, doing it all by yourself and shutting
people out really leads you nowhere.
Yes, you can rise to the top by yourself,
but what good is it to be alone?

A good support system that seeks God and is truly loyal
to him first, will support you truly from their heart.

Although, they are hard to find like a needle in a
hay stack, they are out there deep within.
Keep digging!

To link with a good support system seeks God
diligently to show you who is real.

Make sure you understand and have wisdom in place.
Wait until God builds your support system, don't do it by yourself.
Continue to watch and pray.

In other words two eyes of God are better than one.

No matter what,
know that everyone needs someone, there is no
such thing as "I can do it all by myself".
If you are the one who wants to travel uphill
alone, it is a tough and lonely road.
Get your support system in place and never leave home without it!

Amen
Lady Elease

NOTES – WRITE DOWN YOUR THOUGHTS – DATE _____

_____

_____

_____

_____

_____

_____

_____

_____

FIND A SCRIPTURE TO SPEAK TO YOUR THOUGHTS

_____

_____

_____

_____

_____

_____

_____

WRITE A PRAYER

_____

_____

_____

_____

_____

_____

_____

# Love your hurt

Don't allow it to pile upon you and one day and get so
heavy you can't carry it anymore till it smothers you.

As a child of God you no longer have to carry baggage.
In fact everyday you will have access to the power of
the Spirit of God, the One who "heals the broken-
hearted and binds up their wounds" (Psalm 147:3).

Stop carrying your pain, broken heart, disappointments,
failed relationships, broken spirits and death. Learn to deal
by opening your eyes and see God is reaching for you.

Allow God to love all your hurts away. Trying to
heal or fix them yourself can sometimes become
damaging to your spirit, mind or even health.

If you let God love your hurt the devil will know that he
cannot steal your joy by bringing all these things to you.

When they come you will know how to deal with them.
They are only a part of life and most importantly they are
temporary, so don't hold on to them, pass them over to God.

Keep in your mind that everyone will endure some type of hurt.
What we choose to do with that hurt can only make us
strong not weak or distracted in our walk with God.

God wants us to know he has a provision for our life so
let's start today and allow him to love our hurt.

Amen,
Lady Elease

NOTES – WRITE DOWN YOUR THOUGHTS – DATE _____

_____

_____

_____

_____

_____

_____

_____

_____

FIND A SCRIPTURE TO SPEAK TO YOUR THOUGHTS

_____

_____

_____

_____

_____

_____

_____

WRITE A PRAYER

_____

_____

_____

_____

_____

_____

# Your Prayer Life Is Essential

Let's activate within ourselves
Understanding-Knowledge-Wisdom
They are within each one of us and must be activated through prayer.

Hidden treasures inside us are the wisdom of God,
Building ourselves up by praying in the spirit.
Help us to understand the building up of our temples daily.

Romans 8:26 Likewise the Spirit also helps our infirmities: for we
know not what we should pray for as we ought: but the Spirit itself
makes intercession for us with groaning which cannot be uttered.

Everyone needs a relationship with God. Having
a prayer life draws us closer to him.
This is why your prayer life is essential.

Jeremiah 33:3 – "Call unto me, and I will answer thee, and
show the great and mighty things, which thou knows not"

Never miss a day praying, this is your direct path with God.

The world teaches us that breakfast is the
most important part of the day.
Let me correct you now, every morning when you raise, prayer should
be your first priority, a simple talk giving thanks to the Almighty.

Prayer life will always be essential to your being. Adding a sprinkle of scriptures will draws you closer to God daily.

Yes, breakfast can fill your belly up, however prayer life fulfills the building up of your temple

Get your prayer life right!

Amen,
Lady Elease

NOTES – WRITE DOWN YOUR THOUGHTS – DATE _____

_____

_____

_____

_____

_____

_____

_____

_____

FIND A SCRIPTURE TO SPEAK TO YOUR THOUGHTS

_____

_____

_____

_____

_____

_____

_____

WRITE A PRAYER

_____

_____

_____

_____

_____

_____

# God is not angry with you

Stop beating yourself down thinking your past or
present way of living is causing God to be angry with you.
Your faith in Jesus is your key to unlock the door.
Life for you was bought and paid for.
Stop feeling down and realize that God wants the best for you,
He is not angry with you!
Just because you may be out of order here and there
God has thrown you to the wolves.
He loves you and wants you to get it together.
All you need is to get it right, repent and turn your life over to
Jesus accepting and believing that he bored his life for you.
Everyone has sinned and everyone can get it right.
If you fail trying to live right just keep trying, never giving up.
God is waiting for you, he is not angry.
No one is perfect; just continue on your journey.
God will never be angry, nor give up on you.
1 John 2:1 NIV
My dear children, I write this to you so that you will
not sin. But if anybody does sin, we have an advocate
with the Father--Jesus Christ, the Righteous One.

Amen
Lady Elease

NOTES – WRITE DOWN YOUR THOUGHTS – DATE _____

FIND A SCRIPTURE TO SPEAK TO YOUR THOUGHTS

WRITE A PRAYER

# Welcome to the New

Marvin Sapp says it best in his song.

"So glad I made it,
I made it through
In spite of the storm and rain, heartache and pain still
I'm declaring that I made it through, I didn't lose"

It's a new year, your here,
you made it through.

Take a bow and welcome to the New.

New levels, devils and everything else.
No worries if he helped you make it through he
will help you make it through the new.

There will be good and bad and all you need is to
keep your faith in God to be with you.

Psalm 46:1
"God is our refuge and strength, a very present help in trouble."

Understand you are not doing this by yourself. No matter
who you are remember to always depend on God.

You're in the New and he has brought you over for a reason.

Welcome to the New.

Happy New Year.

Amen
Lady Elease

NOTES – WRITE DOWN YOUR THOUGHTS – DATE _____

FIND A SCRIPTURE TO SPEAK TO YOUR THOUGHTS

WRITE A PRAYER

# Past Incidents

"Remember ye not the former things, neither consider
the things of old. Behold, I will do a new thing; now it
shall spring forth; shall ye not know it? I will even make
a way in the wilderness, and rivers in the desert,"
(Isaiah 43:18-19).

Why do people love to bring up your past?
Better yet, why do you beat yourself down for things you
did or failed at before you turned it over to GOD?

The answer is because maybe you did not completely heal from it.
Every time you hear of things from your past - you
breakdown or maybe Satan knows just what to bring up when
he sees you trying to move forward.

Attention, get over it right now.
Nothing is gone to happen while you sit and dwell
on "why is this happening" or "why me"

There is a cure for the nagging past that will always
try to creep up on your life from time to time.

All you have to do is this;

Keep on keeping, for this is the cure to you sailing through
your dreams, goals and making accomplishments.

I would suggest that instead of running away crying like a baby let your past make you stronger and more determined.

Past incidents are exactly what they say "the past" get over what people are saying and trying to bring up for the downfall of what God has paved for you.

Today is a new day, yesterday is gone and anything in the past is old. No more time for past incidents getting you off track. Get back on the road and when they approach do not detour because God said, "he would make a way."

Amen
Lady Elease

NOTES – WRITE DOWN YOUR THOUGHTS – DATE _____

FIND A SCRIPTURE TO SPEAK TO YOUR THOUGHTS

WRITE A PRAYER

# He knows what's best

I finally know what God wants for me and I know what
I want from God However, if what I want does not fit
in his plans for me its back to the drawing board.

I've been given the free will to do what I want all my life, now
there could be some changes if he does not agree with me.

Uh, I know he knows what's best for me and
if I trust him then I should follow.
So in prayer I shall ask and in mediation I shall wait for his response.

But as for me, I trust in You, O Lord,
I say, "You are my God."
My times are in your hand;
Psalm 31:14-15

To trust God for a great outcome concerning your life you
must take your mind and hands off of it and leave it to him.
Yes, we know that he could have us totally left and we wanted to be
right just keep in your thoughts that he can see what we can't see.
So trust him and wait!

While you are waiting it can be very hard to
understand the path God decides for you.
Don't be dismayed or upset because he knows what's best for you.

Amen
Lady Elease

NOTES – WRITE DOWN YOUR THOUGHTS – DATE _____

_____

_____

_____

_____

_____

_____

_____

_____

FIND A SCRIPTURE TO SPEAK TO YOUR THOUGHTS

_____

_____

_____

_____

_____

_____

_____

WRITE A PRAYER

_____

_____

_____

_____

_____

_____

# Your Temple comes first

Your Temple is so excited when it wakes
up to the presence of the Lord.
Just to think you only set your alarm clock to your favorite
worship song or preacher teaching you the bible. How
refreshing your temple becomes to hear that alarm go off
with worship or teaching. This is going to be a great day.

I remember back in the day I had to wake up to my
favorite song which had nothing to do with worship, if I
heard talking it would be friends cussing up a storm.
Never did I realize that all these things were feeding
my temple with worldly ways. Before I knew it was
a pattern and I yearned daily for a taste of it.

1 Corinthians 6:19-20 ESV
Or do you not know that your body is a temple of the Holy Spirit
within you, whom you have from God? You are not your own,
for you were bought with a price. So glorify God in your body.

If your day is not started off with the correct food which is prayer
and worship you are starving your temple both mentally and
physically. Yes, we feed it nourishment for energy. Is that enough?

Let me answer that for you. No!

Start giving your temple what it needs to have a fulfilled day. The world cannot fulfill your temple, pour a cup of God daily and see how your temple reacts. It's better than food, it's better than people and its most of all it's what you need.

Starts loving your temple today by putting it first, when you do this you're headed on a great path. Remember your temple comes first not your flesh.

Amen,
Lady Elease

NOTES – WRITE DOWN YOUR THOUGHTS – DATE _____

FIND A SCRIPTURE TO SPEAK TO YOUR THOUGHTS

WRITE A PRAYER

# My Choice is Worship

I choose to worship the Lord daily.
In all that I go through my choice is worship.

Why do we go through life situations such as; sickness,
divorces, deaths and loss of jobs to drive ourselves crazy
by complaining, crying and going into depression
when all we have to do is turn it over to God?

Not always in bad times our choices are messed up concerning
worship, it is also backwards in our happy times too.
When we get promotions, married, new homes and cars we
worship that situation and forget all about that God is the
one who made it all possible, until Mr. Bad shows up.

How great you are, Sovereign Lord! There is no one like you, and
there is no God but you, as we have heard with our own ears.
2 Samuel 7:22 NIV

Worship is the answer, at least for me it is my choice.
Instead of worshipping other things by dwelling on
them constantly and giving over control of self we
all should be turning to God in worship.

To worship is so simple, all you have to do is give God the
praise over the good and bad that enters your life.
Open up your mouth with a humble and
pure heart speaking to the heavens.

A day should never go by without worship.
Your choice should be to worship God at all times.
There should never be a dull moment to exalt his name.

I don't know about you but my choice is to worship.

Amen,
Lady Elease

NOTES – WRITE DOWN YOUR THOUGHTS – DATE _____

FIND A SCRIPTURE TO SPEAK TO YOUR THOUGHTS

WRITE A PRAYER

# Walk in Faith

Thinking on God's word when Paul spoke to
us, he said to walk as Abraham did.
Romans 4:3-5
What does the Scripture say? "Abraham believed God,
and it was credited to him as righteousness."
Now when a man works, his wages are not credited
to him as a gift, but as an obligation.
However, to the man who does not work but trusts God who
justifies the wicked, his faith is credited as righteousness.[6]
Life can be a box of chocolates, it will melt in
your hands right before your very eyes.
No matter what is going on never give up
on God, trust him all the way.
So many times when we are trying to do something personally
and professionally things just do not go as planned.
Does this mean walk away or does this mean walk in faith?
It seems we just give up, pout or try something else.
Why not consult God?
Where is your faith?
Why do you just walk away instead of trying harder?
Better yet, why do you have such little faith?
Today is new day, if you read (Romans 4) to get a
complete understanding on walking in faith
you will have a better approach concerning
your daily walk in life going forward.
The only rule to your life is to WALK in Faith,
never look back and trust Gods way for you.

Some things are not meant to work because it is not his plan for you.

Maybe he needs you to totally depend on

him to give his name the GLORY.

As you continue your journey my prayer is that

you trust Gods way for your life,

seeking his wisdom and grace for understanding and believing.


Remember life consist of many hits and misses,

but as long as you stay in the field of Faith you will be okay.

Walk in Faith


Amen,

Lady Elease

NOTES – WRITE DOWN YOUR THOUGHTS – DATE _____

_____

_____

_____

_____

_____

_____

_____

_____

_____

FIND A SCRIPTURE TO SPEAK TO YOUR THOUGHTS

_____

_____

_____

_____

_____

_____

_____

WRITE A PRAYER

_____

_____

_____

_____

_____

May God continue to bless your going and coming?
Do not ever allow a day to go by without seeking and thanking him.
He is worthy of all the praises,
He is all you have
He is your
Fresh Dew
Lady Elease

Made in the USA
Lexington, KY
06 July 2018